D0602666

UNTIL BEFORE AFTER

UNTIL BEFORE AFTER
CIARAN CARSON

WAKE FOREST UNIVERSITY PRESS

First North American edition published 2010

Published in Ireland by The Gallery Press

LCCN 2010922058

ISBN 978-1-930630-51-2

Designed and typeset by Quemadura

in DIN, Engravers, and Walbaum

Printed on acid-free, recycled paper

in the United States of America

For permission to reproduce or

broadcast these poems, write to

Wake Forest University Press

Post Office Box 7333

Winston-Salem, NC 27109

www.wfu.edu/wfupress

UNTIL

BEFORE

AFTER

UNTIL

IT'S THE SAME

old story
but not

as we know
it we thought

it was
a box

until we found
the key on

the verge of
these words

SO IT IS

as when
death draws

nigh death
draws a hush

upon the house
until the one

who is about
to die

cries open
the door

HIS LAST WORDS

were the story is not
over

yet whereof
we cannot

speak until
we hear

the words from
one who has

died
before

whereupon
we begin to

tell what once
was told

ACCORDING TO

the book
of rules that

is he should
not be

his whereabouts
unknown until

he pops
up unexpectedly

alive or alive
as ever

THE GOSPEL

means good
spell if spell

means time
or tell

the story of how
flesh became

the word until
the end of

time when
it decayed

CAST A SPELL

on me
wrap me in

whatever
warp of words

come to
your mouth

until I gulp
them whole

of thought
whatever spin

we enter when
we so imbibe

what neither
had in mind

NOT IN

so many
words not

that I ever
listened

I was that
rapt in

working out
what

to reply
until

THAT FRAME

wherein it
happens who

can say
until that

time has
passed without

our knowing
where we stood

in that blink
our eyes

OF DISCORD

there's a lot
of it about

time or
territory

being
pondered

until it is
broken

by a fell
stroke not

before time
from

beyond once
as before

LEANING INTO

the picture
of a portal

looming from
the fog

so close we
breathe

on it
the threshold

lost until
we step back

WHATEVER

imponderable
toll time

takes we
cannot tell

the order
of our going

hence until
the next

not even
then

WE SEE

the ways
he smeared into

the grey
with his fingers

rubbing out
what paint

had been
until we see

a child
rubbing fog

from a window
with his sleeve

to reveal more
fog beyond

WHAT COMES

to mind
a lull

wherein
words fail

bereft of what
we should

have left
unsaid until

the word
was out

NEXT

as written
in the text

the time is
nigh until you

look to
your life

each day
drawing

nearer next
to nothing

THE CALCULUS

a reckoning
of pebbles

dropped
soundlessly into

a deep
resounding

only in
the memory

until never
happens never

what
you thought

but what
you knew

A QUESTION

about time
the clock stopped

but time
went on

its ways of yore
as people when

one dies do
the story

going on
until told

OF THE CONSEQUENCES

who can tell
the matter with

what went
before what

· happened in what
time or place

reckoning until
the crack

of dawn
as doom

REPEATEDLY

what was gone
comes back

a glimmer in
the fog when

with one stroke
of the bell

the pebble
drops into

whatever deep
will serve

until it comes
to rest upon

a heap
of pebbles

AS GUNFIRE

whips the air
as whips whip

horses to
an onslaught

in the mire
bespattered riders

plunging headlong
until head

to head
heads roll

RECONFIGURED

skein becoming
ball the yarn

spun into what
comes next

a garment
worn until cast

off whereupon
it is unravelled

until ravelled
into skein

CAST

the dice or
knucklebones

a line the hook
or ingot

stitch a vote
the die a gun

the actor to
whatever part

until we look
into each other's

eyes to see
how that cast

of your eye
matches mine

OVERHEAD

a cast of falcons
circles wide

the ground they
eye at random

fathoming
the mine-shaft

of until
when or where

they see then
seize their prey

A LINE

the more
you labour it

becomes
a ball of linen

thread
unravelling

itself to
nothing until

the labyrinth of
this line

of a harpoon
difficult to

withdraw
as in an

anchor fluke
caught in

the jaws of
a leviathan

until hauled
down to

the bottom
ship and ship's

complement are
swallowed

FOR ALL THAT

almost mortal
blow you did

not know
from whence or

why until this
moment

fingering
the scar of what

was what might
well have been

UNTIL AND

of the moment
of your going

hence into
whatever hour

awaits you
you will never

know for all
you know

or know not
not even then

THE HINGE

is what the door
depends on this

I know that
I will not

know until
I find a door

whose hinges
are so super-

naturally
oiled I breathe

these words
upon it

whereupon
it swings

THE HINGE AS HINGES

go
becomes until

between
the one next

and the next
each step

diminishing
the further

on
you go

CREAKS IN THE WIND

a cradle
as the treetops

sough round
its teetering and

so on
until the crack

of doom
the dawn until

forever about
to fall

THE GYRE

that put the gyre
in gyroscope

revolves on
its axis

despite all
external torque

the more we
measure pitch

roll and yaw until
whatever spin

we put on it it
still spins about

its sense of where
it is

I MEAN AN ANEMOMETER

four cups to
the wind

revolving at
whatever scale

it turns it
on to from

low ripple
to high wave or

still in the lull
of until

BY THE BAROMETER

I know the glass
is dropping

slowly in
this lull before

I know
the storm

it seems
to tell that is

not here
until it breaks

is but
a frame

of words and not
the thing

itself if thing
it be

and if
so whosoever

utters it
until it

swings to
has not yet

gone into beyond
the words

NOT UNTIL

your time
has come to

sound you
out from what

lay deep within
you unbeknownst

profound
as any bell will

that sound
take its toll

WHEN AFTERWARDS

you cast
your mind back

to whatever
you thought needed

saying what
comes out is not

what oft
you thought but

afterthought until
this cast of words

A BELL TOLLS

not before time
but dead on

yet reverberating
into the interval

before each next
fell stroke

a ghost
foreshadowing

the aftermath
of sound which runs

on continually
before until

its ever
receding horizon

AT THE COMMA

comes a pause
as if of breath

or lull of time a
sentence suspended

to collect oneself
or recollect until

the word that
went before

the word
that comes next

NOT THE HYPHEN

flitting in
conjoining in

a slip of link
between

an interim
of thought so

brief as to carry
one between

words whether until
to or fro

BUT THE STOP

put an end
to it before it got

to where
the next time

starts so is
both ending and

beginning
what it wanted

to until
it thought

whatever point
it made

that made
it stop

GONE INTO

whatever interim
might lie

in store for him
I say keep

in touch
as we hold

each other until when
at arms' length

I touch his shoulder
he touches me

THE MORE

it's gone into
whether past

or present
future the verb

becomes infinitive
to be as until

that evening of fog
you found yourself in

remains forever
in your mind

I DID NOT KNOW

he'd gone until
now standing

empty in
the empty room

cluttered with
his things some

of which
were mine

or were until
now forgotten

when I lay down
on his bed

into the after-scent
of his aftershave

I WROTE

those last words on
the back of

the customer receipt
deposit slip

he got the day
before yesterday at

thirteen hours two
minutes ten seconds how

long then until
when

AS HE WAS

leaving you
had not long come

back from where
time had stopped

and was only
now beginning

to be incremental
faltering until

both took that step
over its threshold

AWAY IN

the name of a town
many miles away

where he resides
so far away

as back in time
if not in place

uncountable minutes
or years ago

until afterwards over
and over

he would return
to that nameless town

though he had long
abandoned it

ABOUT TIME

no circle
for it cannot be

confined unto
until said

a prisoner in
one of the wards

as of a lock
a key turning in

its imprisoning slot
to free our words

AS IN A WALL

one might behold
footholds

at intervals so many
feet away from

each there is no
next until impossible

to scale a twisted
sheet dangling

from one
shuttered window

THE PAINTER

we imagine
looked at from

the roof or window
of his room while

sojourning in
Naples at the wall

a strip of Naples
blue above

the wall pitted with
scaffolding holes

it would seem
lifetimes ago until

climbing skywards
stone by stone

IN YOUR ABSENCE

wandering from
room to empty

room I do not hear
your silence

in a ward
beyond earshot

time measured
footfall by footfall

drip by drip
until not at all

HOMECOMING

is as yet
indeterminate

depending on
what progress made

on every breath
you draw

bringing you
further on until

little threshold
by threshold

IF EVER

it could be said
to be a box

we found a key
for it but not

as we knew it
the wards

of its lock
turning clockwise

or anti
until something

clicked within
and something gave

an aperture
of daylight

BEFORE

HERE LIES

the road before
that is to all

who went before
the road behind

foreshadowing
our travelling

from twilight
into twilight

mile after mile
time out of mind

THE DAY BEFORE

yesterday if not
the day before

my crossing
over I had all

my wits about
me as for now

where time is not
nor words I cannot say

what might be
foremost in my mind

AN AIRMAN

sees through gaps
in the cloud-

cover the movements
of armies

yet without radio
cannot communicate

as someone who
has passed over

to the unseen world
if such there be

sees what lies before
his loved ones yet

cannot speak
of what he sees

FROM BELOW

a great cloud
roped like

a heavy cable
being slowly paid

by its own weight
before settling into

gross coils
rearing straight up

like
an immeasurable cliff

WANDERING

the underworld
the dead are

like shadows
of their former selves

before we remember
them as well we might

know that they
have forgotten us

not only that
but their likeness

WHEN YOU FORGET

do you get away
from it or it you

does it remain
where you were once

or where you
were when once you

remembered it
before the past

rememberings that
now are lost to it

as ghosts that
wander where

unapprehended they
live out your mind

SINGLED BY

the eye and
taken up by

itself it was
shining white

but taken with
sky

a strong hard
blue as before

a remembrance
of other clouds

WHICH CLOUD

I gazed at lying
on my back

on the green grass
of my back yard

billowing full sail
limned with silver

at its edges
before the clouds

of explosion boomed
from the horizon

THE LIGHTNING

seemed to me white like
a flash from

a looking-glass
but another

noticed it rose-
coloured and lilac

I noticed two
kinds a straight

stroke like the stroke
of a blade

of an oar the other
narrow and wire-like

my eye zigzagging
before them

WHEN IT STRUCK

it was not
before time it was

dead on
the hour limitless

in the depths of
its bell and the full

stroke of its clapper
from steeple beating

out time over
the burning city

LIKE A RAINBOW

spilled in oil
on water shimmering

before you
remembered it

some timeless
yesterday as you

remember it
the more you gaze

into it it becomes
a dark puddle

IN THE PARLOUR

does one look
at who lies there

or take the body
in in glances

no one looking
back the eyelids

motionless
the mouth

sealed as
I look on

him who came
before me

laid out
before me

AS A CONTRAIL

streams from
a glittering speck

traversing the blue
with two fine parallel

white lines marking
time passing it

becomes woollier so
slowly before gone

yet still persisting
the vision

IT IS

as if another city
dark as this one

dwells in this one
as before now that

you hear it through
the helicopter

beat that swells
from where

the city meets
the city

WHATEVER IT IS

I have lost
the credit card for all

I had it in my hand
or had before I

walked away
from it whatever

made me do it when
I go back to

the hole in the wall
I find it gone and

I turn back again
in my remembering

remembering
that forgetting

IN FREEFALL

plummeting
before you

know it not
that you know it

yet from where
you were as if

into measure
after measure

on what scale
not known yet

AS IF

looking into
the body of water

that lies before
you so still as

to be imponderable
until sounding

that deep with
a bell you might

sink a church
steeple in it

IF EVER

twain should
meet as well

we might or
might not travel

measurelessly into
that which was

between what
was and what

was not between
us ultimatum

after ultimatum
gone we still find

before ourselves
ourselves

IN AN ENCLAVE

in an enclave
of a city ward

before a wall
that never was yet

is an enclave
still its borders

understood
by all

who dwell there
notwithstanding all

A NAMELESS BIRD

jetted from its
gorse-yellow nib

an efflorescence
of refrain its

tittering ever-
changing turns

of what it is
perfectly in time

with itself before
it stopped

BEFORE THE STORM

very hot though
the south wind

dappled sweetly
on one's face and

when I came out
I seemed to put it

on like a gown
as a man puts on

the shadow
he walks into

and hoods or
hats himself with

the shelter of
a roof

OR A PENTHOUSE

or a copse of trees
I mean it rippled

and fluttered
like light linen one

could feel the folds of
it indeed a floating

flag is wind made
visible until it snaps

a fusillade
before the storm

AFTER THE FIRST

boom came
another boom before

another boom before
another boom before

how many booms
I could not tell

until they ended
not even then

boom after boom
before boom forever

AS I WANDER

an inner city
street a cloud

singled by my eye
drifts overhead

and I put on
its shadow by

walking into it
as if before into

a cool arcade
I thought long

gone which leads
me to think of what

lost must be
as it is found

I remember
where I was at

the time but
not the time

whatever yesterday
it was before

descending landing
after landing

I landed in
today

AND

is what
comes before what

comes next
and thus is one

of many antes
and is also going

on and on on
time into forever

and thus is never
before time

BACKTRACKING ON

what one
thinks one said

or what one thinks
or thought one

thought was that
said before

the words
in hindsight

now the story comes
out otherwise

the door you walked
through then long

since closed and all
the truer for that

BUT AFTER WHAT

I thought
what time would

it take to do
before it had to be

done if not
whatever that

thing might be
and how it might be

spoken of or to
when gone

WHAT DOES IT SAY

when the lights
dim or flicker

or if before
the lit candles

an organ plays
as if in aftermath

of storm whose music
thunders against

the memory
and that but dimly

BUT OPEN

the book and
look into it you

shall find the words
that are and were

before you speaking of
which the language

is none that you
know or ever knew

yet even so can
spot repeats in

it as one might
jot notes

on a stave looking
for its tune

AS IN A DREAM

stalled by the mind
images swim

between our eyelids
and our eyes until

upon waking and
opening his eyes

one might see
them a step before

him upon the wall
of his room

WHAT THEN

if not now
now that now

has gone that
cloud you looked

at but a fleeting
glance ago

moved on
beyond your ken

to cast its shadow
before elsewhere

BUT NEITHER

the weight nor
the stress of sorrow

by themselves
bring tears

as a sharp knife
does not cut

for being pressed
as long as it is

pressed without any
shaking of the hand

before one touch
striking sideways

and unlooked for
undoes and pierces

HOW IT IS DONE

is to think of
the many as one

as one might be
another not

oneself an army
not a soldier

before one might
be identified

by name or number
if even that

WHEREAS BEFORE

the name was on
the tip

of my tongue if
not at the back

of or before
my mind I can

not now even
dredge up

a face to
put it to

THEY SAID

it was a shadow
quite of what

they did not know
as yet but might

for all they knew
have been there

all along before
whatever turn you

took took you
into what had been

unlooked for until
then so then

they took a knife
to it and took it out

AS BLADE

to haft before
is meet to after

or as one knife
whets another

as is axe
to helve your life

is honed upon
the sharping stone

of what was nigh
a mortal wound

AS SHARP

is to flat
fast is to slow

as fast is
to feast most

is to least
as high is to low

what lies before
now lies behind if

out of sight
not out of mind

CENTIMETRES

I can do without
let's take it

inch by inch
till inch becomes

a foot a yard
or minutes hours

the months before
the months behind

till inching ever
forward foot by foot

you step over
the threshold of

the future that is
over now

IF I STOLE

some things
from you I felt

I was given them
as words are

to each other
when we talk

or one does and
the other listens

repeating them before
they become theirs

WHAT BECOMES

the thought is
how it's dressed

before put on
a cloak that took

so many days
stitching and

unstitching what
becomes what

never was until
it becomes itself

ALL THE WOMEN

sat before on one
side and you saw

hundreds of
headdresses all

alike the hair
made into one

continuous plait
with narrow white

linen not always
the same way

but zigzag lock
and linen

alternating like
rows of regular teeth

S O M E

were dressed in
Italian fashion

with that curious
red and green

diaper border and
black steeple hats

it was that hour
when all the bells

began to ring out
before the storm

AS I CROSSED O'ER I LOOKED

down through
the clouds over

mountains to
a sunlit farmstead

wherein stood
a house a thread

of smoke connecting
it to cloud my eye

swirling as if I'd
entered it before

I LOOKED

upon the road
before me

twilight coming
on the woods

on either side
becoming dark

no traveller but
me upon it

but for him
who walks into

the night and I
his shadow

always watching
over

AS THE SWIRL

in a marble blurs
when it spins

yesterday becomes
tomorrow the day

before its roll
and yaw whatever

spin it took upon
itself to mimic

all its wobble true
as is can ever be

WHAT BECOMES

a boom is what
began not the bomb

itself but the fuse if
the fuse is as long

as it's short as
the day or the year

as the story that
is of before

is told to one
as if of now

IF PRESENTLY

is not before us
where does it reside

if not at present
for the present

as the present city
holds another city

in its interstices
where the hour is

not of the clock
but measured

by indeterminate
distances the distances

by epochs of before
fattening in the now

A BABBLE

of building blocks
bricks and rubble

courses scaffolding
a wall going up

ever skywards
before which you

cannot hear yourself
think for the overhead

helicopter squawk-box
listening in to you

IN THE BOOK OF NOD

it is written
that two ones

were in league
with one another

cleaving each
to each in the bed

of their language
before they split

cursing each other
incommunicably

SO IS

the brain two
hemispheres

what's in between
I cannot fit

which thought
behind to which

before like beads
upon an abacus

dismantled from
their bearings

an incalculable
scattering

of aftermath
before me

AFTER

WHAT BODES

the world to come
is that where

we abide where
everlastingly

the past is not
for all that

has befallen us
we struggle on

embracing this
our afterworld

FOR ALL

my looking
forward after

is not yet nor
then how far

from next it is
I do not know if

next is as in
nearest in time

if not you are
my nearest timeless

ASLEEP

I find you
next to me

for all you
are not here

as yesterday
tomorrow

and today
I walk through

ward after ward
to see you as you

always were
surrounded by

your own space
you allow me into

IN THE LIFT

as I pressed
the button for

Level Three
I thought of

the jolt of
electricity it must

take to get there
and thereafter of

the lift you give
to a coffin

IN THE CORRIDOR

a lady wheeled in
in a wheelchair

old enough to
be my mother

before she died
who after her

admission protested
how dare you come

into my home
this is my home

IN THE REST HOME

the heads of
spectators on

screen
following a long

rally swivelling to
and fro stroke

after stroke for
stroke until one

fails watched
by no-one

I leave and see
a bed left

empty yesterday
already filled

I AM NOT

looked after
this is not

my home where
are my things

I do not
tell her that when

she comes to
leave this home

it will be to
rest forever

I DO NOT

know you gone what
day it is nor how

I got to where it
is tomorrow or

that tomorrow
never comes

what becomes that
interregnum is

when it will be
over ever after

WHEN YOU COME TO IT

you know it
some wall

that strains one
to eye its

seemingly unscalable
height

brushing the sky
to a blue void

whose brink
one teeters on

until one beholds
the scaffolding

holes the scaffolders
left after

ON A SCALE

of correspondences
the words

are weighed
ascending or

descending in
pitch and temper

encompassing
being in time

after which time
is ever thereafter

FIVE BARS

in it takes
a turn into

a darker cadence
that alters how it

began so blithely
before it stumbled

on this scythe in
a field we knew

after all had been
there for all time

WHAT IS IT

is it the it in
electricity

the pulse of
the oscilloscope

monitoring
the heartbeat

as in a spell of
hours

leaving
an after-image

brief as
of

a lightning-flash
switched off

THROUGH SWING

door after swing
door I follow

him until
where he is to

leave me as I leave
well after midnight

it is so quiet in
the hospital I can

hear it breathing
after after after

THINGS

change becoming
after one thing

another if not
this then those

I thought to
bring forgotten

if I ever had
them of no use

in any
case before this

ONE CANNOT

yet say after
all for all

there is to come
we only know

before until
the thing that

shall befall
becomes

another stroke
after reverberating

stroke as of
a bell that tolls

ceaselessly
upon its echo

TIME AND

again time
after time to

play in time
as we did with

each other for
the last time

before now that
after without you

I still keep
your time in mind

FROM A WINDOW LEDGE

between your bed
and the view

of the old jail
restlessly

an oscillating fan
sweeps the ward

as a beam might
the yard searching

after what
is long gone

84

THE EYE

reckons how
many hours

the route from
gutter pipe to

window sill to
overhanging

cornice to
window sill to

parapet to
rooftop ever

after scaling
one's mind

by footholds not
there until

FIGURE

after figure
the minute hand

the hour hand
the bow the link

the swivel
the bolt-ring

the escapement
the analogue

wristwatch at
your pulse

ALL DAY LONG

after gazing
at the cloud

that had not
hanging over

what had been
a prison yard

moved since
yesterday

you watched
the sunflower

the porthole
of the cupola

furnace into
a molten gun

being cast into
a bell that when

founded
would serve

to tell time
time after time

boomed out
over the city

until time
would tell

IS ABACUS

to stave as
number is to note

as in a calculus
of pebble dropped

after pebble
drop by drop

into a well
interrupted echoing

after silence
or not

THE TAG

round your wrist
bore a number

your name
and D.O.B.

two weeks after
two stone less

the day you
came home it

slipped off
no need to snip

WHAT IS

aftermath
if not swathe

upon swathe
of wave before

wave-break
push and

flow slacking
returning

to stress pulling
back clocking

the stones
the beach heaving

with pebbles in
the after-ebb

SUTURE NOT

as in stitching
but a stapling

of titanium
staples by staple-

gun eighteen
of them clipped

to the after-
breach already

healing to the scar
for life

GOING UNDER

is like sinking
into black velvet

after you'd been
told of green

fields the voice
becoming deeper

dusk before
you enter into

the great sleep
of nothingness

COMING TO

is not something
you remember

when I ask you
somewhere

the evening after
got lost you must

have been still
high when

I came to see
you hooked up

to the pulse
of drips through

which I heard you
murmur to me

I WONDERED

where you'd
been these past

hours the space
by my side empty

as I turned over
to find you

not there
in my sleep but

elsewhere after
I thought of it

AS ELSEWHERE IS

wherever we
are not there

are as many
elsewheres

as ourselves
remember how

we meet elsewhere
the after-hours

through which
we played

IT'S ONE OF THOSE

tunes with
a backstitch in it

into its
beginning re-

negotiating what
you thought

it was eluding
you the first time

round the scale
the bridge a gap

you founder into
what you heard

before unstitched
by afterthought

FROM WHOM

we got it hard
to fathom whether

you from me
or I from you

the more we
play it to happen

on other ways
around it ever

changing into
what comes after

TO ENTER

the remembered
portal think

of it as changing
ever after

blue hour to
blue hour

ever bleeding
into that other

city glimmering
within this one

THIS THE HOUR

you look
into yourself if

that is what it is
to be alone if ever

that without you
I still see

you as hooked
to the life-

supporting apparatus
you looked at

me as I looked at
you as you

smiled for
the first time after

OF ASSIGNATIONS

there are many
if not one

behind the city
in the city

where one
stranger meets

the other both
shadowing each

other hour after
hour forever

EAST OF EDEN

lines drawn
in the sand

rank and file
of pebbles laid

therein to stand
for ones and

tens and hundreds
calculation done

wiped clean thereafter
till tomorrow

THE NEXT TUNE

in as it goes
as follows is

as the one
that goes before

the one after
you change it into

as we had always
done until it

slips our minds
as if from bond with

but one glance
we change as one

into another one
the same one

FROM BEYOND

a boom
the window

sending waves
into the room

a cloud above
the city as we

turn to face what
it might be to

behold it bloom
after boom

HOW MANY

seconds does it
after the aftershock

take how many
years to take before

we know what
target it might

reach that
secrets might

be breached
after that what

THAT I MIGHT KNOW

tell me what it
is like beyond

the bell that beats
at one and you

come after one
who came before

if not then
very like as these

two hands as you
the traveller

returns as word
would have it

is it then like
as they say

FROM WHAT

elsewhere am I
summoned up

to tell of what
it is you ask

that I unfold
one thing after

another not
knowing where

I come from nothing
is except before

THIS IS THE DAY

we learn how
it is how it

will be the after
cast already

cast the runes
being read

upon the screen
before our eyes

take in what
must be taken in

·SO FAR

and yet so near as
in one throwing

pebbles at
an unanswered

window where
shadows move

upon the blind
as if after each

other I were not
there imagine

how much more
difficult it is

for the living
to get through

WHAT IS IT

this parabola
the pebble

describes as
in a word

thrown at one
by people hail

the pebble
after pebble

parable
or babble

IT HAPPENED

once upon
a time if not

after when
what was to

tell was told
as sling to

stone or scythe
to spell

of time to
what was mown

THE TURN

you took abroad
the turn you took

at home we never
knew might turn

to this the aftertime
of what

has been and yet
it is as one

might turn
a tune another

way and find what
one or other

never knew the tune
beyond the tune

THE TUNE

is what we
know we think

we know as
blithely we

begin until
a stumble

brings us ever
deeper in

to aftertouch
resounding

I NEVER

thought that it
would come to

this the after-
knowledge of not

knowing then what
it would bring as

if it could be
otherwise

since otherwise
is what we are

TEACHING ME IT

you break it
up into where

one phrase turns
into the next not

what I thought
I heard but

what I heard
slowing it

down into
note after note

before note
repeating it until

I play it after
you until with you

YEAR AFTER YEAR

playing the tune
over you've been

cutting out
the frills getting

to know how
the notes are more

truly told by
leaving them

alone to be
found by the bow

YOU ONLY

knew the first
part before from

the ice cream van
chimes that

always died after
it as it would

stop until
one day you heard

it turn thinking
of going home

I OPEN THE DOOR

into hall and
over threshold

after threshold
slowly oh

so slowly I bring
you heavy

step by step up
the seventeen

steps of that
flight once trodden

so swiftly as
year over year

to our room
full of light

ACKNOWLEDGMENTS

Some of the poems depend on the terminology of Irish
traditional dance music, where the first part of a tune is
often called 'the tune' and the second part 'the turn'.

Some of the poems in 'Before' have been lifted verbatim or
with some modifications from Gerard Manley Hopkins' prose
journal as in *The Journals and Papers of Gerard Manley
Hopkins*, edited by Humphrey House and completed by
Graham Storey, London 1959. They are as follows:

'From below', 'Singled by', 'The lightning':
p. 212, July ?, after July 8, 1871.
'Before the storm', 'Or a penthouse': p. 233, July 22, 1873.
'As in a dream', 'But neither': pp. 194–5, Dec. 23, 1869.
'All the women', 'Some': pp. 172–3, July 12, 1868.

Some of the poems were suggested by my reading of
China Miéville's novel *The City and the City*, London 2009.

I am grateful to Tess Gallagher for her editorial suggestions,
which led me to revise some of the poems; and to Guinn
Batten for comments on the work in progress, which led me
to write poems I might not otherwise have written.

The first six poems in this book were published first in *Many
Mansions*, published by Stoney Road Press for the Ireland Chair
of Poetry. 'The tag' was published first in *The New Yorker*.

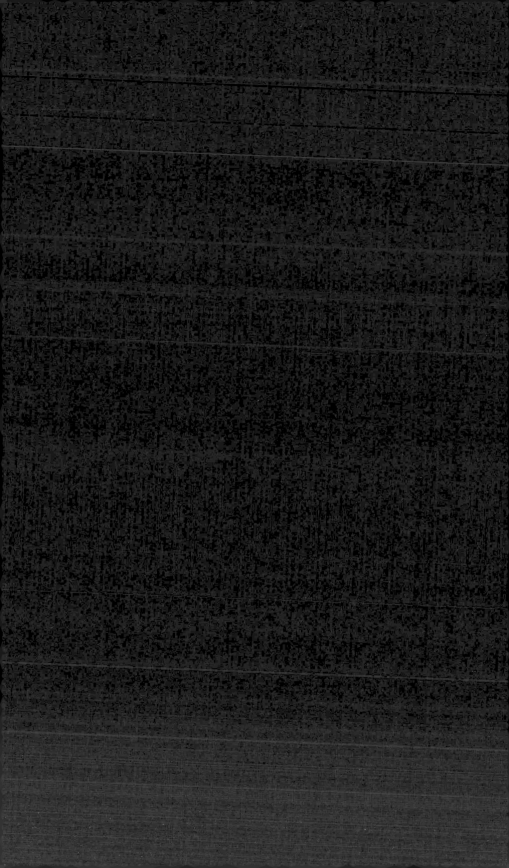